I0790506

CHANGE

"For those who are too hard on themselves."

MAHA ESSA AL A ANZY

authorHOUSE

AuthorHouse™ UK
1663 Liberty Drive
Bloomington, IN 47403 USA
www.authorhouse.co.uk
Phone: UK TFN: 0800 0148641 (Toll Free inside the UK)
        UK Local: 02036 956322 (+44 20 3695 6322 from outside the UK)

Published by AuthorHouse 05/05/2021

ISBN: 978-1-6655-8886-7 (sc)
ISBN: 978-1-6655-8887-4 (e)

Print information available on the last page.

Any people depicted in stock imagery provided by Getty Images are models, and such images are being used for illustrative purposes only.
Certain stock imagery © Getty Images.

This book is printed on acid-free paper.

Because of the dynamic nature of the Internet, any web addresses or links contained in this book may have changed since publication and may no longer be valid. The views expressed in this work are solely those of the author and do not necessarily reflect the views of the publisher, and the publisher hereby disclaims any responsibility for them.

CONTENTS

Do not ever think that motivation will appear in your life like that. Motivation won't appear until you take the action (don't wait to FEEL motivated before you take action).

Whether that means completing your 30 minutes' workout then taking a shower to leave your house for work or perhaps telling yourself to read the book you've always wanted to read. The motivation will follow you and you won't realize how much you've accomplished.

What actions can we take to generate motivation? It all depends on the action you take to keep that motivation cycle working for you. It's all about knowing how to react to things during the difficult times.

And keeping motivators around your work area – things that give you that initial spark to get going. These motivators will be the triggers that remind you to get going.

It's okay if you don't know how to motivate yourself you can always learn.

Here are some effective ways to motivate yourself:

Try something new today.

Make a to-do list.

Start exercising, and you'll feel like yourself.

Have a reward system, so you'll have
something to look forward to.
Get the hard stuff done first thing in the morning.
Eat right.

CONFESSION

I've always wanted to write a book like this journal, but a lot of people have let me down and made me feel like I wasn't good enough to do so. Those setbacks are nothing because no one stops you from doing what you like! I thought maybe because English is not my first language but I believed that I could do it. I tried so many times but never finished one. This time I decided to challenge myself to deliver the story. I have to for the people who are struggling to move on with life. People who are stuck somewhere in the past. There are hard times in life. I believe that every struggle we face teaches us a valuable lesson that we will never forget. I believe that what we have been through in the past is the reason where we are now. I believe that if life gets tough, we get tougher. I believe we are able to do anything in this life but the problem is the people we live with. Why? Why can't we all just be happy for each other, support each other, motivate each other? It's a pathetic world we live in but guess what? People will never change. They will always find ways to let you down. So, don't give a fuck about what people, say or think. You keep on doing you no matter what. Keep your energy as high as you can and make sure that happiness is your first priority. And let the world know who you really are. Most important thing when reading this book is to believe in yourself, believe in the person you are and believe in every possibility you have.

~Life has away of pushing our dreams away ~
~The key to hit destine is to reach your dreams ~

READER

Alright, let's start off by telling me, how are you feeling. How are you? No, I mean really how are you? I know that a lot of us are struggling with things that are not fair in this life, like mental health struggles, relationships, bad situations or maybe just a struggle at work, but hey it's ok not to be ok sometimes or even if you don't know how you really feel seriously it's normal! Those of you out there who are consumed with fear, consumed with worry, don't worry. It's a confusing world out there, but it's on us to look for peace and answers to our questions, solutions to our problems. Remember that God loves you and will always protect you no matter what or how bad it gets. Everything will pass. Why worry when God is here? Why worry when everything is written for the better? Don't fear the future because God is here and will protect your tired worrying soul. I can talk about my struggles and fears and sins too but, I don't define myself with those battles. I fight back against them because it's the only way through. Don't let the devil and his confusion inspire you to climb a place you can't get out

Everything is going to be just fine.

CHANGE

First love yourself into change. Use some compassion with yourself and notice that your unhealthy behavior is an alert that something is not right in your life. Love yourself enough to make some changes don't wait until you hit '' rock bottom ''to make the change. Most bad habits are in reaction to stress: Over worrying, loss, avoidance of tough situations. These types of stress can destroy us. Therefor change becomes hard and challenging. choose something to replace your bad habits, remove triggers. take baby steps if necessary. Put effort on you, focus on you, work on yourself to transform your life.

Believe that you will have the strength and courage and determination to get things done, to change what needs to be changed, to change your perception about certain things, to change your identity, in certain ways, to transform those things that are outdated: outdated beliefs, outdated viewpoints, outdated knowledge and education. Expand your life and relationships, expand your energy. {maybe true happiness is when we are happy with ourselves}.

Change like the weather, change for the better, and remember the sun will always shine again. Change is everything we need, it's everywhere, even in nature. There are two types of change, "seasons change" and "sudden change like storms." The idea of change can be unsettling. A lot of people would like to avoid changes regardless of whether they are huge or little. Nonetheless, change is a fundamental piece for our self-awareness venture and generally ought to be embraced. Change contacts all parts of life, however accepting change in your profession, (for example, taking a [PRINCE2 project the board course]), can contribute gigantically towards positive self-improvement is (change is hard at first but beautiful at the end) trust me.

This year I decided to challenge myself by changing all my bad habits to good habits. Who doesn't have bad habits? Let's all agree that we all do, but the difference is how you deal with them and whether you let them affect your life or not. I have a lot of bad habits to change physically and mentally, habits that are slowly draining me draining my energy. One of the bad habits I've been struggling to change within me is that I've always had these bad or negative thoughts about anything, like talking negatively to myself, this didn't only lower my self-esteem but also made me second-guess myself all the time which I hated. It is like expecting the bad before it even happens. It reached a level where I started defeating myself instead of uplifting myself. Most of us think that this kind of self-talking won't have an impact on us, but the reality says that it has a huge impact, especially on our mindset on the people around us and everywhere we go we bring the bad energy with us. It's draining and tiring to have this kind of mindset nowadays.

Certain circumstances can make you feel a little bit down about yourself. I don't know what you're going through right now but what I do know is that you can change anything you don't like. Within you mentally, physically and most importantly intellectually that you have no control of but don't let the negative talking, the bad talking control you. I'm not going to tell you how to change it but what I'm going to tell you is from my personal experience I've decided to challenge myself to make this change not only for myself but for all the people in my life the people that I work or live with, I think the worst thing ever is to start your day so depressed, sad and that you have to go work and bring all the energy to people you work with.

There's no such thing like a negative thought. When you have or start thinking negatively replace that negative thought with something positive. For instance, if you hear yourself say "oh

I look so pale and ugly without makeup" immediately replace it with "my skin looks nice and glowy for my age" or "I'm stunning I look sexy today." So, instead of saying "I know I can't do it" say "I will do my best" and instead of saying "I can't be constant" say "I will try to change, one step at a time" instead of "I hate my life" say "I love how I'm living my life."

If you can't do this and come up with a positive thought, come up with solutions to your negative thoughts. so instead of "I look pale" or "I look ugly" follow up with "it doesn't matter as long as I eat well and take care of my skin". thinking about these solutions might help you think more positively. Not only about losing weight or looking healthier. But life in general. One thing that helps you change a lot of things. Is to stretch yourself beyond your limits every day, because you have more potential than you think but you will never know your full potential unless you keep challenging yourself everyday Pusina past your own self limits.

Learn from your own experience, if you had a bad day, sit back and review it, learn what went wrong and how to avoid it the next day if it happens again. don't let a bad moment destroy your whole day. don't neglect yourself, get things don't do not let neglect destroy you, learn how to control small disciplines before god gives you bigger ones to learn from the smallest disciplines.

INNER VOICE

"Don't shush your inner voice"
It's who you really are.

Be more aware of your inner voice. The voices we all have, our thoughts and our inner voices or guts feelings. The voices that either lifts us up or push us down. Our mind is a very fascinating thing. It regulates so much of our different experiences in life; how we perceive them and how we react to different things. Hence, you can almost say that the world actually goes on inside our minds, and not really outside, when you think about it. Stop thinking that you messed up, your true feelings will never ruin something real.

There's this feeling I carry everyday of success, that reminds me of everyday, even if I'm having a bad day. I know for a fact that I will be something unimaginable in the future. it's like I have this image drawn in my head and I look at it everyday so that I don't settle until I'm there. If you don't do the things you're supposed to do, to change¬ improve, or own, no one would, if you don't talk to yourself every morning and motivate you, no one would, if you don't talk to yourself about success and all the things you can do no one would, if you don't remind yourself of who you are and what you're capable of no one would. It's very important to do all these things for you. It's very meaningful

<u>Repeat this daily</u>

- I AM AMAZING
- I CAN DO ANYTHING
- I AM PREPARED TO SUCCEED

Why your most important relationship is with your inner voice?

Your inside discourse shapes mental prosperity, says therapist Ethan Kross. He has the instruments to improve your psyche's backchat. As Ethan Kross, an American exploratory therapist and neuroscientist, will merrily affirm, the individual who doesn't now and then wind up tuning in to a pointless voice in their mind likely doesn't exist. Ten years prior, Kross wound up sitting up late around evening time with a slugging stick in his grasp, hanging tight for a fanciful aggressor he was persuaded was going to break into his home – a figure invoked by his wild psyche after he got an undermining letter from an outsider who'd seen him on television. Kross, whose region of examination is the study of reflection, realized that he was going overboard; that he had succumbed to what he calls "gab". Yet, revealing to himself this did nothing but bad by any stretch of the imagination. At the pinnacle of his uneasiness, his negative musings running fiercely on a circle, he got himself, fairly cleverly, Googling "guardians for scholastics".

Kross runs the superbly named Feeling and Discretion Lab at Michigan College, an organization he established and where he has committed most of his vocation to considering the quiet discussions individuals have with themselves: interior exchanges that effectively impact how they carry on with their lives. Why, he and his partners need to know, do a few group profit by going inwards to comprehend their sentiments, while others are well-suited to self-destruct when they participate in unequivocally a similar conduct? Are there good and bad approaches to speak with yourself, and assuming this is the case, are there procedures that may helpfully be utilized by those with internal voices that are only a tad excessively uproarious?

As the years progressed, Kross has discovered responses to a few, if not all, of these inquiries, and now he has gathered these discoveries in another book – a manual he expectations will improve the existences of the individuals who read it. "We're not going to free the universe of nervousness and wretchedness," he says, of Babble: The Voice in Our Mind and How to Saddle It. "This is anything but a glad pill, and negative feelings are acceptable in little dosages. However, it is feasible to turn down the temperature a piece when it's running excessively high, and doing this can help we all deal with our encounters all the more adequately."

As indicated by Kross, who converses with me on Zoom from his home in a blanketed Ann Arbor, there now exists a hearty assortment of exploration to show that when we experience trouble – something X-ray filters recommend has an actual part just as a passionate one – participating in reflection can do "fundamentally" more mischief than anything. Our contemplations, he says, don't save us from ourselves. Or maybe, they lead to something tricky: the sort of negative cycles that turn the particular limit of people for reflection into a revile as opposed to a gift, with possibly grave outcomes both for our psychological and actual wellbeing (thoughtfulness of some unacceptable sort can even add to quicker maturing).

Does this imply that it's not, all things considered, great to talk? That those in treatment ought to quickly drop their next arrangement? Not by and large. "Staying away from our feelings in all cases is certainly not something to be thankful for," he says. "Yet, we should consider distance all things being equal. A few group compare this word with evasion and restraint. Yet, I consider it the capacity to venture back and reflect, to broaden the focal point, to get some viewpoint. We're not keeping away from something by doing this, we're simply not getting overpowered."

Those who are able to quieten their inner voice are happier; their sense of relief can be palpable

As indicated by one investigation, we converse with ourselves at a rate identical to talking 4,000 words each moment (via correlation, the American President's Condition of the Association address, which generally rushes to around 6,000 words, endures over 60 minutes). No big surprise, at that point, that tuning in to it very well may be depleting, regardless of whether it appears as a meandering aimlessly monologue, or a urgent reiterating of occasions, a free-acquainted pinballing starting with one idea then onto the next or an enraged inside discourse.

Yet, on the off chance that such clamor can be incapacitating, it can likewise act naturally undermining. What we experience within can scratch out nearly all the other things in the event that we let it. An examination distributed in 2010, for example, shows that inward encounters reliably predominate external ones – something that, as Kross notes, addresses the way that once a "ruminative" thought grabs hold of us, it can demolish even the best party, the most ached for new position.

For what reason do a few group have a stronger or more alarming inward voice than others? "That is more earnestly to reply," he says. "There are so numerous ways it tends to be enacted, some hereditary, some ecological." What is sure is that these encounters can't be limited: "The information is overpowering with regards to the association among nervousness and actual medical issue." The individuals who can quieten their inward voice are more joyful; their positive feeling can be obvious.

What is intriguing about the science engaged with this is the way it the two backs up, and conflicts with, instinct. A lot of Kross' book is given to what he calls the "tool compartment" of methods that can be utilized to dial down prattle, and keeping in mind that a portion of these appear to repudiate all that we think and feel – "venting", for example, can do an individual more damage than anything else, in light of the fact that discussing negative encounters with companions can regularly function as an anti-agents, driving away those you need most – others affirm that when we follow up on specific impulses, we're all in all correct to do as such.

To take one model, in the event that you are the sort of individual who slips into the second or third individual when you are in a fold ("Rachel, you should quiet down; this isn't the apocalypse"), you truly are benefiting yourself. What Kross calls "separated self-talk" is, as per tests he has run, one of the quickest and clearest methods of acquiring enthusiastic viewpoint: a "mental hack" that is inserted in "the texture of human language". Conversing with yourself like this – as though you were someone else by and large – isn't just quieting. Kross' work shows that it can help you establish a superior connection, or improve your exhibition in, say, a prospective employee meeting. It might likewise empower you to reevaluate seemingly an inconceivability as a test, one to which, with your own support, you might have the option to rise.

Dream big, accomplish more, set goals.

When you close your eyes, what do you see? what comes to your mind? do you see yourself stuck in routine overloaded with things in which you see no purpose in doing in which you have no interest in. are you a victim of your own past and circumstance?

When we are mentally burdened, our brain responds by interpreting the overload as a physical threat and our stress response system goes into high gear. I believe we all have a breaking point, and it occurs when we reach a point of despair. being at your breaking point is not necessarily a bad thing if you can use it for an impetus for positive change. Paula Morand, CSP a leadership speaker says that It's amazing how when allow our negative emotions, situations and even our own bad behaviours a place in our life it can wreak havoc in so many ways. It tears down relationships, impairs your confidence and disrupts decisions and dreams. If not tackled, one can easily stay in a place of acceptance of "what is", resulting in a low self-confidence, feelings of inferiority, loneliness and deep loss. I call this the cycle of our own choices as we alone have the power to make choices to move out of it… starting with the perspective of how we choose to see the situation. I believe everyone can break the cycle and get back to dreaming big and being bold in their life. We all have the power to make the decision to let go of dreams not fulfilled, reframe them and take control of our pursuit of dreams not yet realized. The first step is to stop holding yourself back. Let go of the stress that is debilitating your decisions and rather turn that overwhelm into the fuel that will propel you forward. The combination of dreaming plus action… and I mean massive action will keep you moving forward. It's not one simple step but many little things that add up to big results. Dream big and be bold! There is no other way but to just start!

Sadly, we live in a society nowadays where people hate to see successful people have attained heights which everybody dreams of. So there can be many reasons to hate successful people; People think they were less capable of success and some people think they themselves are more deserving. Some think God is unfair. Some are just fed up of trying and failing and again trying and ultimately hate the successful Also one of the reasons is that those who are close to you and are successful, they actually make you feel much more jealous than the unknowns. Personally, I don't hate them, I learn from them. Never underestimate anybody successful, even if they're complete idiots and most people think so, there is always something about that person which makes him /her successful i. e. always think they know something which you don't

All you have to do is to put in work, focus instead of sitting doing nothing, make yourself busy, have a vision of your life, Practice self-love because it's you feel strong. In fact, it's the strongest thing you can do for you. love yourself. find out your soul's desires. say to yourself I'm gonna take control of my life and progress it. {learn to work hard on yourself then you do on your work}. When you work hard you make a living for you and your family, but to work on yourself you make a fortune wishes super powerful. You can attract anything.

What we do wrong that makes us forgot our dreams and goals? What I do I wrong is I don't champion myself enough to have a good start we always put people first. I do tend to put people first and ask myself how with other person feel which makes me put them first all the time some peoples are what I like to call emotional vampires people that are complain too much about their problems they always suck the life out of you by listening to them moaning and complaining about everything in their life never thank for Anything. in order for you to succeed you have to cut those people out of your life at some point and learn how to be alone sometimes how to be able to get out of any conflicts and how to de- escalate them out of your life as to carry on with your dreams.

People face conflicts every day but it's not about how hard it gets it's about how you get out of that conflict and make the conflict small D escalate the problem and carry on with your life.

CLARITY

Clarity is power. The clearer you are with what exactly you want to be or become the easier it is to reach your goals and desires. Be clear, be specific, be strong. Define what you want and, and work for, embrace it, believe that you're capable of reaching your goals Make a dream become reality. Lack of clarity can cause you confusion. When you're lacking clarity you can never be certain about anything you can never be settled, and we manifest that as anxiety and confusion.

How to avoid uncertainty? You must have a plan. have a clear path so you won't need to change plans more frequently. so if you define what you want you work towards it. goals will become like a magnet and pull you to their direction. The direction of reaching your goals. Another way of avoiding lack of clarity. Is to be comfortable with choices you make, because if you don't you'll doubt your ability of reaching that goal. And second guess yourself this will make you uncertain and you can never be relaxed because of those questions. Don't ever doubt yourself because really you can do anything.

It's very important to be clear about what you want in life. To be clear about your relationships, your work, your life and your goals, you have to have a clear image for your goals, and dreams to make them true find your way through and start going. Find what is it that you really want and start digging your way through it. Once you are clear about your objectives and goals, it's simple to accomplish them. The vast majority don't have clear goals Notwithstanding, if you want to make progress towards your goals and be successful in life, you need to know precisely what you need to do. Without defining clear and unequivocal goals you won't center your energies and would not achieve a lot.

How to achieve your goals in 10 steps

1. Take actions
2. Try harder
3. Keep practicing not quitting
4. Find new ways
5. Ask for advices
6. Do your very best

7. Learn how others did it
8. Build your strength
9. Review and fix mistakes
10. Don't ever give up

OVERTHINKING

Overthinking will fucking kill you.

It's likely that overthinking causes mental-health problems. overthinking is linked to psychological problems like depression and anxiety. Overthinking kills your happiness. Did you know that 98% of your problems would be solved if you stop overthinking things? Just breathe calm yourself.

Why do we overthink everything?

We overthink because we are desperate creatures hunting for answers. We like certainty and we like being in control. Don't worry, it's part of the human survival tactic. Well, somewhat. Overthinking is not all bad. Probability theory requires that all possible outcomes of an event must be explored to determine what can really happen in that given situation. We know what that is like; before a big event we find ourselves thinking about it so much, we create hypothetical beginnings and endings and even climaxes of said event before it even happens. In a way, it is preparation, so that we can deal with whatever outcome there is and not suffer from too much of a surprising consequence. And in a way it is vaticination. We cannot predict the future, but there is a deep longing inside of us that wishes we could have. Our intuition gives us half ability to do that. This way, we sometimes can sense when something is wrong, where we should or should not go, who we can and cannot trust. We have a powerful inside voice us that can sometimes save our lives. Overthinking puts that voice on blast. It is a harsh process to go through but it is sometimes necessary.

Overthinking is fear.

Fear is a seed of a treacherous tree. We were not born with fear, it came upon us either through imparted lesson, life experience or trauma. Unfortunately, we had little to no control over what was taught or done to us in the years of our childhood. Many of us still have branches of fear living inside us from since the days of our youth. Things happen to us in childhood, relationships, friendships and in jobs and the ugly part of the experiences latch on to us so tight, the thoughts about these past experiences surface like settled poison oozing through the brain in a single moment of "thinking too much."

We form these destructive thought patterns that are almost inescapable once we begin. We think and think about something that might be a completely innocent situation, but it is because the poison has erupted and infiltrated our minds, we create this hell. The more we overthink, the more fear we invite in and the more unsettling our thoughts become. It is a vicious cycle especially to those who suffer from anxiety disorder, depression and even suicidal thoughts.

Signs that you're an overthinker:

- can't stop worrying.
- often worry about things I have no control over.
- constantly remind myself of mistakes.

- relive embarrassing moments in my mind over and over.
- often ask myself "what if." questions.

Why do we overthink everything?

Our biggest obstacles in our life are often found in our own mind, but the truth is not everything our mind thinks about is true! Your mind is the most powerful force you can ever have in your life, because your mind lies. it will tell you, you can't do this, you can't do that, you're not ready enough, you must thank it for its opinion and move on.

Fact: Did you know that overthinking is the biggest cause of unhappiness. Keep your mind off the things that change your mood, things that don't help you to move on things that leave you

How to Stop:

It is impossible to completely erase fear. You cannot just "let go of fear". Meditation will help you silence your thoughts and develop patterns of clearer thinking but you will never be able to erase fear. Why? Because fear is part of human instinct and it is necessary in that aspect of survival and avoiding danger. However, very rarely or perhaps never will we find ourselves in front of a tiger, and we have to make the decision to either run away or become its meal. Fear then, has the power to outsmart the mammal or even kill it. Stress and emotional fear is different. Fear that attacks our emotions is harder to class as a fear that is helping us survive. So, all we do is overthink. We give into that type of fear and it stresses the brain to the point of irrationality and in some cases, insanity.

How do you stop?

Pay attention.

Train yourself and your mind to be more self-aware. I have stickers on my vision board in my workspace that says "be aware" and "stay focused" and as trivial as that method seems, it helps. The moment you feel yourself about to drift off into "overthinking land", you can do two things; either **be completely silent** or **start talking.**

ESCAPISM

The necessity of escaping is essential during these hard times. Reality can be tiring at some point as many people may feel overwhelmed sometimes so a little escape can be healing. Sometimes the stresses of the world can make us just want to scream. The constant of bad news or negative thoughts and our counties connection with our devices make us feel trapped with Strong desire to escape. Sometimes I wish I never existed, I wish that I had a superpower that would make me disappear whenever I want to. Maybe we just need some time alone to control ourselves and Let it be. When we have this kind of feelings it may be that our minds and souls are sending us signals. We are being reminded to take a step to take care of ourselves and start healing it. Most people would escape reality for a certain amount of time. It might be that we crave physical or emotional Escape.

Five years ago, I used to never take care of myself and be there for myself. I was always busy with a lot of things happening in my life. At work I never missed a day. I was always on time and sometimes I go earlier then I should. I was always there whenever my friends needed me. I was busy with everything in life, but I was never busy for myself. I was always around people which made things a lot harder until I realised that all I needed was to be alone for a while to get back on track through my mind and focus which was hard as a results of this unhealthy lifestyle. I used to get angry and confused so quick and found it so hard to focus on one thing. Sometimes on my head I needed to escape the reality I was living in but I didn't know how. I kept pressuring myself and refusing to heal it. And that's what I call unhealthy reality of life style. So I need the healthy escape to make my way through life. Because No one would want to live in an unhealthy life form.

The first think I needed to do is considering this type of escape is to clear my mind. Clear my mind of the daily negativity that I was going through the daily clutter. One way that really helped me clear my mind is engaging in meditation focusing on my breathing more. Practising yoga this is perfect, yoga has many health benefits but mainly it focuses on relaxation encourages you to focus on the presents. And on your breathing, it also manages your nerve system. Overalls yoga is brilliant to restore your power and energy again to be able to clear your mind. Another way I found very helpful for a healthy escaping is to listen to music. Music is A healthy form for escaping studies have shown that music increases your self-esteem and help you relax.

Daydreaming

It is so beneficial. Allow yourself to daydream which is the perfect mental escape. Dream that you're somewhere else. In another planet or another world, maybe just another country. Sometimes I dream that I have my own island. I dream that I have a small tent that I sleep in. I eat coconut in the morning. There are a lot of nice fruits there. The island is in the middle of the beach or the ocean when no one knows me and I don't know no one. I do dream that I take a swim in the ocean whenever I want to. This type of Daydreaming allows me to forget reality for a certain amount of time and enjoy dreaming. I find it very relaxing. I believe that I will have my own island somehow someday. Make daydreaming a habit that you maintain for as long as possible. The good time for daydreaming when you're working out the daily routine or when you're cleaning. Reading and writing is an absolutely great way for escaping. Reading helps you enter into a whole new world and escape reality.

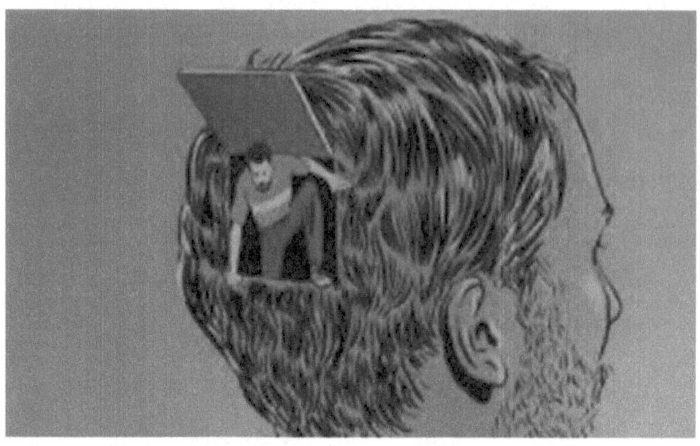

Remember It doesn't matter which method you take. Fuck this message. It will depend on the reason you wish to escape. What are your escaping from, and results you would like to achieve?

Psychological escape

Freud considers a quota of escapist fantasy a necessary element in the life of humans: "[T]hey cannot subsist on the scanty satisfaction they can extort from reality. 'We simply cannot do without auxiliary constructions', Theodor Fontane once said". His followers saw rest and wish fulfilment (in small measures) as useful tools in adjusting to traumatic upset; while later psychologists have highlighted the role of vicarious distractions in shifting unwanted moods, especially anger and sadness.

However, if permanent residence is taken up in some such psychic retreats, the results will often be negative and even pathological. Drugs cause some forms of escapism which can occur when certain mind-altering drugs are taken which make the participant forget the reality of where they are or what they are meant to be doing.

Does escaping means running away from dealing with your problems?

You cannot just keep floating through life and never deal with the issues. There has to be a balance in knowing when to escape and went to face your problems and fix them rather than running away from them. At the point when we try and escape we might be attempting to try not to invest energy with ourselves. Escaping can be something contrary to care. Escaping permits us to numb ourselves to a reality we might not have any desire to acknowledge. Similarly, as critically, if not more in this way, ongoing escaping hazards distancing us from companions, family and others.

Examples of bad and good escapism.

Good escape

The good kind is when you escape from a narrow world into a broader one. You allow your mind to take you where your body, for whatever reason, cannot go. You refuse to accept the shackles of external circumstance and exogenous suffering, and you cultivate freedom and adventure in your own heart. The bad kind is when you escape from the possibility of a broader world into a narrower, "safer" one. You live in your mind as a way to avoid taking the difficult action your body could. You refuse to acknowledge that your shackles are the result of internal issues and self-imposed suffering, and you feed delusion and distraction in your heart. The first kind helps us ascend the pain of this world. The second kind prevents us from doing the hard work necessary to grow. Escaping pain outside your domain of control is elevating. Escaping the pain inherent in self-betterment is debasing.

MENTAL HEALTH

It's always good to sit and think back to times when someone has helped you in whatever way. This could be, when you're in an unfamiliar place and someone showed you direction or someone has explained something for you as you've been struggling to understand. These things are quite general. And I suppose we all have had at some time in our lives had to reach out for a little help. But I sometimes think back to a time when life wasn't so good for me. My life, through a lot of problems became very difficult to cope with even when small asks of people were massively hard for me.

In 2016, I lost my only true friend. like any loss of a person, especially a friend. but through the complexities of life, most of us carry on, however general, but with the burden of loss with us. I was working from 6 am until 9 pm everyday. In some way, my hurt and pain was hidden by the work, as I wanted to forget at least 10 hours ahead. and obviously I didn't just switch off my brain to not think about the pain.

I was going through but it helps when you keep yourself busy with something. I wish our brain had a reset button to forget. If there was, we would live in an emotionless way just like Robert programmed us to do things without feeling the pleasure or pain of life.

In 2017, my mum was sick along with other personal problems I had in my family. I couldn't not believe it. I had completely gone to the lowest I would say I could go. I also couldn't see any more points in life. Getting up in the morning was my biggest struggle. It felt like my body and mind died inside of (me). Though, I was still too scared, my feeling, of how, why, when all the times of this hurt and pain was making it worse. I wasn't able to be any use for anyone anymore.

I took my mum to her hospital appointment once but I wasn't allowed inside with her. So I sat outside in the waiting area. waiting and wondering what was to come.

All of a sudden, I heard someone steps coming towards me, closer and closer. I looked up and it was an old lady who came to say " hello ". I wasn't in the mood to talk, but although I looked up and answered respectfully. I assumed she was just a patient. She asked me so politely if she could sit beside me. She started introducing herself and asking who I was. I responded, although truthfully, just wanted to be alone but I couldn't. I had to be respectful. She asked me if I was waiting to be seen or if I was waiting for someone and if I wanted coffee, (she was drinking one) I said '' no thank you '' then she asked a few more things about where I'm from etc. Was in away of care. I felt like she genuinely wanted someone to talk to; she seemed happy talking to me. 20 minutes later a doctor came to tell me about my mum. He seemed very careless and cold. However, this woman was the opposite she was very caring and asked about my mum like she knew us.

She simply put her hand on top of mine, ''smiled and said your mum is going to be fine, she's lucky to have a caring daughter like you, my daughter would never come to my appointments with me ''. Her hand on my hand, her words literally cost nothing, but it meant a lot to me. Before this, I felt like there was no one to talk to, all I wanted was for someone to hold my hand for a moment and acknowledge how I felt. 'A small act of kindness can make a big difference in someone's world.'

What is mental health?

According to World Health Organization (WHO), mental health is defined as "a state of well-being in which the individual realizes his or her own abilities, can cope with the normal stresses of life, can work productively and fruitfully, and is able to make a contribution to his or her community". As we all know mental health can affect daily living, relationships and physical health. They also emphasize that preserving and restoring mental health is crucial on an individual basis, as well as throughout different communities and societies the world over. In the United States, the National Alliance on Mental Illness estimates that almost 1 in 5 adults experience mental health problems each year. In 2017, an estimated 11.2 million adults in the U.S. or about 4.5% of adults, had a severe psychological condition, according to the National Institute of Mental Health (NIMH). A lot of things can cause us to have mental health problems nowadays especially with what is going on right now in the world with the covid-19 and the lockdown all these things have an impact on us. It can impact your studying progress. Your mental health in general depends on it. The pressure it puts on us is very heavy. There are so many types of mental health.

Stress

Events that put pressure on us; for example, being told to do something in a very short time, when you don't have enough control of what happens. Reaction to being placed under pressure, that feeling we get at difficult times. Professionals often disagree over whether stress is the cause of problems or the result of them. Try to manage external stress because difficult situations do not appear all the time. It can develop your emotional resilience. Try and cope with hard times /

situations when they do happen and don't be hard on yourself don't think you're way too stressed.

While I was writing this book, I was going through stress and anxiety, an unexplainable way that I felt unexplainable. It felt as if I was lost in the middle of nowhere, like my soul was stabbed but it's not showing from the outside. I would get very angry and calm in seconds, no one can ever imagine the pain I was going through. That stress I carried in my soul for so long has taken over me over my energy, though I couldn't function. I kept asking myself everyday is it normal to feel that way, I knew I was going through so much (family issues), (work), it maybe a results to how I was feeling. it left me very feeling less towards a lot of things. A matter of fact I couldn't cope with it, but day by day stress have developed anxiety, anger, mental health. I became an unknowingly strange and hard to deal with. I knew this was not me I attempted to change so many times but failed attempted to cope with stress and anxiety but I failed.

After so many days of trying and failing again, I decided to accept it, accept the fact that I have it and yes it's affecting my social life but I embraced it, embraced the sudden change that has happened to me. After a while I was getting closer to the person I was before. I started a new job in a school, kept myself busy with things I like such as; music, writing, reading, meeting friends, it was all a matter of time, and a matter of accepting yourself with all the sudden changes that may happen. Don't let stress take over you, take over your strength and ability of doing things. Life has a way of teaching you things, battling you to see if you're strong enough to beat it or lose. It was all a matter of time; time heals my friend.

Anger

According to a recent study by sociologist Ronald Kessler at Harvard Medical School, this anger disorder is on the rise, and may be present in more than fifteen million people. And this is only the proverbial tip of the iceberg. By definition, an Intermittent Explosive Disorder, "the degree of aggressiveness expressed during an episode is grossly out of proportion to any provocation or precipitating psychosocial stressor." This is precisely the case in so many of the mass shootings in recent years. But a difference is that some reportedly have no prior history of aggressive episodes. Typically, the perpetrator, often described by friends, family and co-workers as passive, polite and quiet, is triggered by some insult, rejection or stressful event, running amok on a vengeful rampage to restore honor or repay the injury to his fragile ego. Some cynically and nihilistically seek recognition, attention, infamy. But, in any case, their violence is a gross overreaction, a devastating nuclear detonation of pent-up aggression, anger and rage. Why?

He believes that we are seeing a similar pattern in most of the other diagnoses traditionally applied to such angry, aggressive, violent individuals. Oppositional and Conduct Disorder are manifestations of underlying rage. The depressed, irritable mood and often furious manic behavior of Bipolar Disorder have deep roots in unconscious anger and resentment, as do the hostility, temper tantrums, rage and aggressive acting out in Antisocial, Borderline and Narcissistic Personality Disorder. Indeed, I tend to consider all these diagnoses variations of anger disorder, and believe it is crucial to explicitly recognize them as such.

Anger disorders describe pathologically aggressive, violent or self-destructive behaviors symptomatic of and driven by an underlying and chronically repressed anger or rage. Anger disorders result primarily from the long-term mismanagement of anger, a process in which normal, existential anger grows insidiously over time into resentment, bitterness, hatred and destructive rage. Anger disorders may also be caused or exacerbated by neurological impairment and substance abuse, both of which can inhibit one's ability to resist aggressive, angry or violent impulses.

But, for the most part, anger disorders cannot be blamed on bad neurology, genes or biochemistry. They arise from a failure to recognize and consciously address anger as it arises, before it becomes pathological and dangerous, starting in childhood. Who is to blame for this failure? We are. To the extent our society condemns and denigrates the effect of anger as negative, worthless or evil, ignoring and denying its positive potentialities, we are partly responsible for the subsequent carnage. To the extent that mental health professionals continue to avoid confronting anger head on in our patients, choosing instead to try to drug, behaviorally modify or cognitively rationalize anger away, we clinicians too are compounding the problem.

How to treat anger?

Think before you speak. It's not difficult to say something you'll later lament. Take a couple of seconds to gather your considerations prior to saying anything — and permit others engaged with the circumstance to do likewise. When you're quiet, express your displeasure. When you're thinking plainly, express your disappointment in a self- assured however calm manner. Express your interests and needs plainly and straightforwardly, without harming others or attempting to control them.

Exercise

Being active can help diminish pressure that can make you become furious. On the off chance that you feel your displeasure raising, take an energetic walk or run, or invest some energy doing other agreeable proactive tasks.

Identify possible solutions

Rather than zeroing in on what made you distraught, work on settling the current issue. Does your youngster's untidy room make you insane? Close the entryway. Is your accomplice late for supper consistently? Timetable suppers later at night — or consent to eat on your own a couple of times each week. Advise yourself that outrage will not fix anything and may just aggravate it.

Depression

It is a condition that can affect anyone at any time in their lives. Although many of us have experienced our moods fluctuate from time to time, sometimes feeling sad, upset or even fairly low, when feelings like these persist and you find that they overwhelm you, affecting your daily responsibilities, you might be suffering with depression.

Depression is a very unpredictable sickness. Nobody knows precisely what causes it, yet it can happen for an assortment of reasons. A few people experience sorrow during a genuine clinical disease. Others may have despondency with life changes like a move or the demise of a friend or family member. Still others have a family background of gloom. The individuals who do may encounter sorrow and feel overpowered with trouble and forlornness for no known explanation.

What Are the Main Causes of Depression?

Abuse

Past physical, sexual, or emotional abuse can increase the vulnerability to clinical depression later in life

Certain medications
Conflict
Death or a loss
Genetics
Major events

How did I get over my depression?

Six years ago I suffered from high-function depression. The signs and symptoms of high-functioning depression are similar to those caused by major depression but are less severe. They may include changes in eating and sleeping habits, low self-esteem, fatigue, hopelessness, and difficulty concentrating. Symptoms persist on most days, causing a nearly constant low mood that lasts for two years or more. Most people function almost normally but struggle internally.

I wasn't able to function in one or areas of life. I was not able to hold down a job, couldn't perform academically, used to always avoid social activities, for example; my family and relatives used to gather every Friday to have dinner and enjoy a nice friday together I used to always avoid seating with them. I would find a place where I could sit alone and avoid talking to them because not wanting to come to the family dinner wasn't an option. I could be forced to go sometimes. same as my relationships never was able to keep a healthy one among many other potential areas. There are other symptoms I have experienced like overeating then not eating at all the next day. felt so sad and hopeless. I hated making any decisions as I found it hard to concentrate.

The first step I took was getting the right help. From my personal experience I believe that getting therapy is very essential if you suffer from any type of depression. It taught me how to recognize negative patterns in thoughts and to actively change them. So, getting help is very essential because treatment can make life more enjoyable. As it improves your mood, improves your functioning and leads to better outlook and quality life in general. It is very important to check if you are adopting any negative thinking traps and try to replace them with positive or neutral thinking. Don't even give yourself time to think negative if you do instantly replace it with something positive. Write down how you feel, and why you feel that way, at the end of the day review it, read it and consider any of your negative thoughts was truly justified. imagine the incident again in your head and think from other perspective.

Do the things you like doing. Find out what truly makes you happy and write them down even if it's something you did in the past. push yourself to do even one of them at least. even if you don't feel like it. you may be surprised of how it's going to make you feel after. engaging in activities you love more frequently, improves your mood gradually.

Where ever focus goes energy flows

Have you ever been so excited about something, but didn't know how to do it? something you give a lot of emotions to, so it became part of your life. it could be love, relationships, body transformation, something that you don't just vision it's in you. Well whatever that something is it won't happen without you putting the work in it grind towards it because vision it it's not enough.

Work, work, work, take every possibility to, work hard, train your body, train your mind, you don't have to be the most intelligent to reach your goals. You don't have to be smart to change your life. The only thing you need is to work on yourself. When you look at the people around the world, no one was creative enough, rich enough, disciplined enough, intelligent enough to become what they are now. It's do or die, swim or drown, challenge yourself. Talk to yourself positively, motivate yourself and become the best version of yourself for yourself.

Take an extra distance, push further, don't stop when your body's screaming doesn't stop. Everybody wants to do great things in life but they don't put in the work sacrifice for something. nobody wants to be phenomenal, it's the process that makes you see it.

I had a choice to make. I asked myself, do I have the right reaction or the bad reaction? I always have a why. I kept looking for someone to choose for me. then I said to myself why do I always seek help from people? why am I not enough for myself to choose, to make decisions on my own. people have absolutely no power over me. Don't be defeated, get yourself up and work, keep moving, cry if you must, but don't ever stop.

TRANSFORMATION

We all want to be something better than we are. You're doing the right thing but the bad thing happened. That's exactly me all the time. it's hard to make the right choices when the wrong thing keeps happening. I know how that feels, late at night is the time I feel sorry for myself, I found out the hard way is what happens. You fail all the time, but don't embrace it, because it's not alright to lose, it's not alright to give up, if you don't fail you're not even trying. The question is what are going to do with what you have? I was 20 years old and I was at my lowest. until one day I was at work like normal, this old man I used to work with said "Young lady, you're very kind and nice to talk to I can imagine you with a bright future. You have the prettiest smile always do you, be you, and don't settle for less, if you're not happy with something change it, you deserve to be happy." What he said left me speechless. He was such kind person.

Sometimes you barely make progress and that hard situation makes you want to stop. I know that you could be going through a lot of tough situations but don't stop. No matter how hard the situation gets, don't let the idea of quitting drive you crazy and quit but guess what if there's no pain there is no gain. Keep working no matter what even if the progress your making is barely progressing. Don't allow that inner doubt to tell you that you can't do it because the hard time you're in does not determine you. Think differently, see things from different perspectives. We have been damaged emotionally, spiritually, mentally. it's not what you go through that will detriment who you are. It's victory not defeat. It's opportunity not giving up, it's getting better not worse. You can do anything if you put your mind into it. whatever it's you're doing, do not give up on yourself the only thing that can stop is you. They say you are born alone and you die alone. fight through this battle through whatever you are going through. fight your way through life, fight your way through divorce. Fight your life through anything you're battling with.

Take every single opportunity you have right now because you're still living and make an impact on this world. do not give up on your life because once your life is over you can't come back. If you don't struggle, how would build strength how far are you willing to take? Your life is your life. When life gets tough you get tough, keep living strong. Life is definitely worth living. you cannot wait for somebody to make your life better. You have to be prepared for anything that life hit with and face it. You believe in everything in the world but you don't believe in you?

Be the strength for someone when they're weak.

Being kind to the wrong people

Do you ever feel so lost? Like you can't feel anything, care to do anything, you just exist. I was lost in my own head in this crazy wired life. I felt like I was emotionless, cold hearted, had a lot of questions that needed to be answered. I cried every night without knowing why. I always wanted to scream but at who? You know that feeling of burn in your heart when you cry. I felt like that everyday, as if I was missing something so precious, missing something in me. I wanted this feeling of sadness and pain in my heart to go away, I was falling apart and I knew I wasn't depressed or anything like that.

I thought, maybe it's the people around me, their fakeness and how careless they can be has left me questioning myself. I was never treated well like a wife, a lover, a friend. I was never enough. Why though? I never got an answer until I decided to not give a single fuck about how people feel and why they treated me like that, I knew that I was more than enough. I was always there for them and that shows me that

I was enough. I decided to do the right thing. I changed my attitude and way of talking around people and spoke very less only if I was asked to, I would help if help was needed, not more not less. I figured that people will never appreciate what you have to give them. There is always a time where they will beat you up for your kindness. People will never stand by your side. These kinds of people made me learn a lot of things and change a lot of things too. I've learned how to deal with them, I've learned how to be there for myself, fight and be strong for myself and not be taken advantage of.

I changed how I treated them, yes, but I'm still the same kind person. I will always be, and I'm proud of it because I know there are people like me out here always been kind to the wrong people. Always there for people, but no one is ever there for them. Never change being a good person for the wrong people. Your behaviour says everything about you and their behaviour says enough about them. But instead learn how to control your emotions around them, don't be too kind, don't be too easy. Treat them exactly how they treat you. It doesn't matter how bad life hits you, what matters is you get up stronger so that's when it hits you again you won't fall down. always fight back for your rights, stay the way you are no matter what, and take care of you because no one ever will.

Karma says what goes around comes around. Set boundaries with people and exactly how you wanna be treated.

I don't usually regret a good move I make in my life. But sometimes I regret being nice and apologizing when I didn't do anything wrong and for making unworthy people a priority in my life.

GIVER

I've been a giver my whole life.

It's always give, give, give but never receive. I've been a giver in everything literally, love, life, money, friendships, feelings. At first I felt so good to give everything even if it was the last thing I had. I felt good at first because I knew deep down that I'm a good person. I hated telling people " no " even if it's the best, but I just hated rejecting people. no one ever thanked me for what I've done for them no one ever said that I'm kind to them despite all the sacrifices I've always given to them. It was never enough or I wasn't enough. Everything has an end, a full stop, no matter how far it goes, or how far it goes, or how bad it gets. Don't ever be there be for someone who has ever hurt you, used you, hurt your pride.

It sucks to give everything you have for the sake of love. I used to say to myself "I'm a good person, why do I get tread so bad," "Why am I not appreciated for what I do?" "Am I enough?" until I felt so bad about giving and that's when it all started. The problem was I didn't know or I wasn't taught to say "no."

I sacrificed a lot of things which I wasn't supposed to. I was always looking out for others until I realised that it is not okay to be taken advantage of all the time. It's not okay to say "yes" for the wrong people. Giving away your values for the wrong people who never appreciated who I was, people who took advantage of my kindness are the worst people ever. I realised I was wrong when I stopped giving. when there's nothing left to give, there was no one around! That's what made realise that no one deserves your kindness, no one deserves your sacrifices.

Learn how to say " no " to people. I'm not telling you to start rejecting people and say no all the time. I'm telling you to know when to say it and when not to. I used to say it all the time so I've been used to it. I hated how I would feel if someone told me to know so I didn't want anyone to feel the way I felt, but I was wrong most of the time. There comes a time where you have to stop crossing the ocean for people for people who wouldn't jump puddles for you. Since I stopped giving, caring, loving, I haven't heard from a lot of people in a long time, it's like they never knew me.

You must be asking yourself how do I stop being taken advantage of?

It's very simple, just set limits because takers never do. Be more selfish, add value to your life first, add self love and peace to your life first.

Be nice but learn to say " no. "

Relationships / Don't give something you will lack.

Sometimes when we are hurt by someone, we don't give ourselves time to heal. When you allow yourself time things heal faster. Sometimes we get hurt, we break our own heart in a relationship and we rush so quickly to the second one without healing ourselves. And then the next thing you do is you get hurt even more this time. It's hard to process the hurt. Sometimes think of a scar in your hand. The first thing, it will burn you so badly, you try to cool it down and let it heal by time you won't try to get burned the same way on the same spot on your hand you will give time to heal until it disappears.

Don't invest yourself in the wrong people because when you invest in yourself in the wrong people they will break you into pieces and torn you apart in such a way that it takes years to get back together. You break your own heart by making somebody more important to you than you are to them. Simply put, if you don't want your heart to be broken over and over again by someone do not let them back into your life because you have history together. If your relationship went from something beautiful to chaos, let those memories go. Accept that the past will never be the future. Stop going back to what your heart is trying to heal from.

Have expectations in your relationships. For example, are they willing to give back the love you have to give them? Are they worthy enough? Are they showing enough? Are they capable of being someone that is going to be in your life? Because it's an honor for someone to be with you to be in your life. Because you're vulnerable enough. You are worthy. You deserve the best relationship ever because you love people deeply. You're trustworthy and kind. do not let anyone change those expectations ever just because you love them it doesn't mean that they can treat you like shit and you accept it because you love them. It only means that they don't love you enough in fact they never have. Because love it's a very beautiful thing and not so many people miss understand it. Love is respect it starts and ends with it. Love means respecting and accepting the person as they are.

-Don't invest in your emotions in the wrong people

When you love someone way too much but they don't share the same love with you, because simply they don't admire you as much as you do for them. That will make you think that you're not enough for them and want to do anything for them to love you more, so you start loving them more to meet their needs so that they can like you again. But that's going to make them eventually dissolve you because you are always there when they need you, you don't let them miss you, have their free time to think about how they mistreated you, or even a chance to love you again.

If it ever gets to this point, where you give everything you got to make someone love, share the same love with you if you have to do all the hard work for someone who doesn't even want to be loved like that, leave them! let them know your worth. Don't beg to be loved or treated nicely. You deserve to give and receive love in the same exact way. Leave them because you know your worth. You value yourself enough to not beg them for it. Leave because in love you're not supposed to beg it. You're not supposed to let go of all the things you like just because you are that person. It's very important to have exceptions when it comes to relationships. Don't lack emotional intelligence. Some people can be so desperate to be loved because they don't love themselves enough. You become more lovable if you love yourself enough and believe in it.

Don't be too needy, know exactly what kind of relationship you want and how you want to be treated.

It all begins with you, love yourself enough if you want to be loved.

Being kind to the wrong people

I have never been this sad and lost before. It's like I didn't feel anything I just existed in. I was lost in my own head in this crazy weird life, felt like I was emotionless, cold hearted, had a lot of questions that needed to be answered. I cried every night without knowing why, I always wanted to scream but at who? you know that feeling of burn in your heart when you cry. I felt like that everyday, as if I was missing something so precious, missing something in me. I wanted this feeling of sadness and pain in my heart to go away, I was falling apart and I knew I wasn't depressed or anything like that.

I thought, maybe it's the people around me, their fakeness and how careless they can be has left me questioning myself. I was never treated well like a wife, a lover, a friend. I was never enough. Why though? never got an answer until I decided to not give a single fuck about how people feel and why they treated me like that, I knew that I was more than enough. I was always there for them and that shows me that I was enough. I decided to do the right thing. I changed my attitude and way of talking around people and spoke very less only if I was asked to, I would help if help was needed, not more not less. I figured that people will never appreciate what you have to give them, there is always a time where they will beat you up for your kindness, people will never stand by your side. These kinds of people made me learn a lot of things and change a lot of things too. I've learned how to deal with them, I've learned how to be there for myself, fight and be strong for myself and not be taken advantage of.

I changed how I treated them, yes, but I'm still the same kind person I will always be, and I'm proud of it because I know there are people like me out here always been kind to the wrong people, always there for people, but no one is ever there for them. never change being a good person for the wrong people, your behaviour says everything about you and their behaviour says enough about them. But instead learn how to control your emotions around them, don't be too kind, don't be too easy. Treat them exactly how they treat you. It doesn't matter how bad life hits you, what matters is you get up stronger so that's when it hits you again you won't fall down. always fight back for your rights, stay the way you are no matter what, and take care of you because no one ever will.

Karma says what goes around comes around. set boundaries with people and exactly how you wanna be treated.

I don't usually regret a good move I make in my life. But sometimes I regret being nice and apologizing when I didn't do anything wrong. and for making unworthy people a priority in my life.

SELF-VALIDATION

We rely on others to make us feel good. We doubt our abilities if we're not explicitly told we're doing well. Depending on outer approval can make us angry or depressed. An absence of self-assurance may make us raise more mistakes and have hell concentrating. Also, dissatisfaction and analysis are particularly difficult on the grounds that we put such a lot of stock into others' feelings.

We can't depend on others to make us feel better. At the point when we do, we permit others to direct our value. Furthermore, we don't confide in our own contemplations, emotions, and decisions; we accept others realize more than we do and their sentiments matter more. We become needy and ask for validation in ways that turn others off – in ways that scream my self-esteem is lacking and I need you to tell me I'm okay.

You are not insignificant in this world. Remember all the little things you do to make others notice you. Someone adores the coffee you make them every morning and gets out of bed excited to drink it. Maybe a joke you said to someone once and they laugh every time they remember it. Someone loves themselves a little bit more, because you complimented them. Someone reads the book you recommended and changed their life from it. So, never think that you have no influence on people whatsoever. Your good deeds can never be erased.

You are deserving You are influential You are appreciated You are loved

4 steps to validate Yourself

1. Notice how you feel and what you need.

   Example: I feel angry. I need time alone.

2. Accept your feelings and needs without judgment.

   Example: It's okay to feel angry. Anyone would feel angry in this situation. Taking time alone will help me sort out my feelings. That's a good thing.

3. Don't over-identify with your feelings. We want to accept our feelings and also remember that they don't

define us. Notice the subtle, but important, difference when you say I feel angry vs. I am angry or I feel jealous vs. Our feelings are temporary – they come and go.

4. Remember, practice is an important part of learning self-validation!

Essence of self-validation

- Try not to judge yourself (this will typically lead to shame)
- Allow emotions
- Practice being you
- Treat people the same way you want to be treated
- Appreciating yourself is a great way to feel valid and important in any moments of your life.
- Loving yourself more will allow you to feel loved and cared for by people you love around you.
- Loving yourself does not make you selfish in any kind of way.

Validating and loving yourself means?

- Accepting yourself and not worrying about some mistakes you've made.
- Being honest with yourself.
- Taking advantage of all your strengths and beating your weaknesses.

- Be unique in your own way, don't fake things you can't do.
- Be proud of yourself.
- Believe in inner strengths and in your existence.

Once you learn how to love yourself, you will know your true worth and importance in this life. Knowing true self love and expecting bad and good advantages, you'll be able to learn love and act like it without feeling forced to or responsible to do so. If you truly love yourself, you'll see life in a different image you will see the beauty of it. Despite the hate and ups and downs in life, you'll feel grateful and connected for it. Remember true love is self-love.

We criticize ourselves for many many years, but it doesn't help, does it? It never worked. We should try approving ourselves and see what happens. if you don't give yourself the right validation that you need, you will be trapped trying to seek it. You don't need anyone's or anything to approve of your worth. Don't let anyone minimize how you feel. If you feel something, you feel it and it's so real to you. no one, invalidate that ever. they are not you, they don't live in your body, don't let anyone judge how you feel, your feelings are important, they deserve to be heard.

SOUL HEALING

What is soul?

soul=spirit=information =message

Soul healing is an energy healing system that may be similar to Medical Qi Gong, Reiki or Healing Touch, with one major difference, Soul healing is healing at the Soul level that goes even beyond energetic or physical healing. You don't have to be fully healed to give or receive love again. Spend time with yourself, learn how to love and heal again and carry on living.

How can soul healing help with physical, mental or emotional conditions?

All healing and sickness begins at the level of the soul. This concept is recognized by many ancient and modern healing modalities. At the soul level there is a spiritual reason for everything that occurs in our lives. Blockages can occur in our physical body causing pain and illness, in our mental body causing stress and other issues, in our emotional body creating unbalanced emotions and in the spiritual body creating blockages to our spiritual journey.

Protect your heart at all costs.

One way to prevent yourself from getting hurt is to be in a relationship with someone for the right reasons. For example, if you're in a relationship just because you are afraid of being alone, this will leave you heartbroken in the future because you're not invested in that person. You will be searching for someone else to meet your needs. Juliana Breines, Ph.D. says, "Given the importance of social connection to our well-being, it is understandable that we seek out intimate relationships, but when fear of being alone drives our romantic decisions, it can lead us to exercise poor judgment and to choose relationships that are unlikely to last, that make us depressed or even leave us vulnerable to abuse." To have a meaningful, long-lasting relationship, you must be comfortable with yourself while believing that you truly deserve happiness.

Find your inner peace and heal your soul.

It could be anything that makes you simply happy or relaxed. This is a way to heal yourself from anything that's hurting you or even a bad energy. The thing that makes me happy is music. Maybe it's the only way I can get out of a stressful day at work, or a fight with someone. Listening to songs I like can change my mood instantly. Another thing I like doing is writing and colouring. Colouring is a good way to let bad energy free. There are different types of soul healing

I want you to write things that you consider soul healing

1.
2.
3.

And then pay attention to how it'll make you feel after.

The moment I knew I was healed.

The moment I knew I was healing, when I took a road when I didn't think or want to invite anyone. When I didn't feel the need to listen to music because my own thoughts were enough company, when someone asked what I was doing on a Saturday night I said " nothing without needing to justify myself. I still have moments of sadness but once I started looking for moments of joy I started finding them everywhere. we need to find moments of joy to carry us through the tough times. Enhance our ability to keep moving forward in constructive and positive ways. You may think " okay, I can see why it is important to find a moment of joy in the time of sadness, but how do I exactly do this, when I'm feeling so down? "

First, you have to allow yourself to feel joy - say it to yourself"
I deserve to feel happy ", " I deserve to feel joy ", " I'm aloud
to feel it " or even write it on a piece of paper and repeat it
everyday. This will help you be more able to be happy and
experience joy.

Next, think of an exercise you like: meditation, focusing
on your breathing more, it can make a whole difference
when you're feeling down. Know that sadness is temporary.
find a way to laugh and to cheer yourself up, maybe watch
your favourite funny show or movie. Therefore, laughter can
be especially effective if you had a stressful day at work or
feeling frustrated with something. Surround yourself with the
people you love, family members and friends can be the best
medicine when you're feeling down or stressed. Sometimes
all you need is someone to listen to you, and give you some
positive thoughts.

I've always look for something, maybe a place somewhere, or
a special night, always looking for a nice sky view, for sunrise,
for the moon, and the sunshine, for a book, for a song, for
colors of the rainbow, for rain drops that reminds me of
something, for a story, or white blank sheet so I can fill it up
with words and feelings that I feel towards all those things.
I heal around those things. I heal from a hug or nice honest

opinion from someone you like. The small details that attract me, attract my soul.

How depression has affected me.

I've suffered from high-functional depression and excessive stress for a long time. And the only way I got out of it was through support groups and finding connections. I always find something to look forward to and live for. When I'm down, I search something interesting and write about it. For example, I've always loved the idea of working at a police department so I always search about it and all the job role they have there. This would make me feel better and then I put it on my calendar or maybe plan a party with friends -whatever brings a smile to your beautiful cheeks again.

How it felt like.

At some point in my life, I've been struggling to focus on anything. It felt like I was floating without swimming, too confused to focus, I had all the time in the world but my brain just refuses to. I could get very annoyed if someone tells me to concentrate on something, I try to focus but I find myself day-dreaming instead. I could be getting into a deep conversation with someone and at the same time I'll be thinking about ten other things in my head! or, I could be reading something like a book, and I find myself thinking about what I would wear tomorrow? I hope someone can relate to me.

Lack of focusing was a big struggle to me. It reached a point where I was always wondering about almost everything. The books I read, sometimes I read it twice just to understand it because I wasn't focused when I first read it. Crazy right? But it's normal to not be concentrated all the time and losing your train of thoughts. We rely on concentration through almost everything in life, your performance at school or work can be affected if you can't focus. A lot of things in our lives can be the reason for our lack of contraction. I knew it was serious when I couldn't think straight, when I hated making any decisions, I let people decide for me, which was very wrong but I couldn't, when I could never sit still for a second. I thought I was tired. But even when I sleep enough hours I struggle as my body feels knackered after long hours of sleep. So I thought that it can't be lack of sleep or tiredness. I've spoken to my doctor about it and he advised me to follow a balanced diet plan with whole grain vegetables etc. which wasn't very helpful. As well as reducing caffeine intake. I used to drink about 5 to 7 cups of black coffee a day, which led to my shakiness and increased heart rate.

I came up with some changes that helped me be able to improve concentrating more. (From a personal experience)

Things that can help you focus more:

1. Reducing caffeine
2. Eat more healthy / follow a balanced diet plan
3. Exercise 30 minute a day if you can/dancing
4. Meditation
5. Writing /reading
6. Walking

~The power of meditation ~

When you're single minded, you are one dimensional, your mind becomes narrower and narrower and narrower, and remains focused on one point. This is concentration.

Meditation means the mind has stopped. You are pure consciousness, simple awareness; all the dimensions are available to you so it's just the opposite of concentration. " Osho"

FACT:

Depression is a diagnosable and treatable condition. so don't ever think that you live with it your whole life. There are many ways you can get out of it.

The real definition of life.

- To achieve, and to feel competent

- To fulfil our sense of autonomy and control
- To be emotionally connected to other people and part of a larger community
- To have a sense of status within social groupings
- For privacy and rest, to reflect and consolidate learning
- And yes – to have meaning in one's life

Meaning becomes difficult, if not impossible, to achieve if these needs are insufficiently satisfied. Unfortunately, modern society seeks meaning to life through materialism, to the detriment of our biological needs, leading to dissatisfaction and a consequent inability to find meaning. The result is an exponential increase in mental ill-health. Sadly, then, many of us will not experience the satisfaction of a meaningful life journey.

How to control your life.

I know that a lot of us struggle with that. It could be the circumstances we are under or maybe things that aren't working out for us, and we decide to just give up. Let me tell you one thing, if you don't control your life yourself, life will control you, decide for you, hurt you, make live under its circumstances, because you're not bothered to live right. You don't mind your younger friend, sister, cousin, choose for you, tell you what do to! Because they will see things from their point of view. They maybe ignorant or maybe hate you.

Don't let people decide for you because it's your life your, own life. They don't struggle with you or deal with things the way you do, right? There's nothing wrong with taking an advice from someone else, but it's wrong if you let them choose your future for you. Why don't you work and control yourself for you? Work on yourself and believe that the world change for you. Quit chasing, trying to fix everyone's life. Focus on you for you and you'll be surprised how the world around you will change so dramatically. You're enough for you to change and control your life.

They feel overwhelmed by life. They struggle to make choices and decisions. They often feel stuck, adrift, or thwarted. It's incomprehensible not to be influenced by everyone around us—it's not difficult to "get" their feelings, for instance, and our minds tend to synchronize up when we partner with others. That implies you should define limits with troublesome individuals, unravel yourself from negative online associations, and be more aware of how you may be defenseless against "oblivious conformity"— pressing factors to act or think in manners that are in opposition to your qualities.

Instead, surround yourself with friends, family, and communities who encourage you to reach your full potential, nurture your talents, affirm your values and difficult decisions, and give you a reality check when you've behaved badly or are stuck in negative thinking. You can also get involved with your community through volunteering or just chatting with local merchants or neighbors. These positive social interactions will improve your state of mind and physical health, two critical building blocks of agency.

Move

Physical movement, along with proper rest and nutrition, puts your body and mind into balance, giving you greater motivation, strength, and stamina. Research has shown that sitting a lot is dangerous for your health, and that even short breaks from concentrated periods of inactivity—like getting up to stretch or walking around the block—are good for you. Studies also suggest that exercise can lead to greater self- control—the ability to defer gratification, which is key to agency. If you're in deep at work, set a timer to go off every hour and remind yourself to take a moment to assess your mood. If you're feeling stuck or overwhelmed, get up and move. And, if you're having any issues at work, discussing them in a walking meeting (instead of a sitting meeting) may help mitigate conflicts.

Position yourself as a learner

People with high levels of agency are continually learning more and expanding their capacity to learn by adopting a more open, collaborative approach to everything in life. This requires nurturing your curiosity and allowing yourself to explore new ideas, skills, and people. You can take an interesting class, explore your world kinetically (through your hands or body), or spend time playing or using your imagination. Or you can learn from other people by staying curious and asking them open-ended questions, listening to gain understanding, and avoiding any quick judgments. This isn't always easy. Practicing a growth mindset—where you recognize that you are a work in progress, capable of learning and changing—can help combat the fear of failure or judgment that often come with learning new things. If you have trouble letting go of perfectionism, it might help to practice mindfulness meditation, which has been shown to reduce self-judgment, or use cognitive-behavioral therapy techniques that help put mistakes in perspective.

Manage your emotions and beliefs

Too often, we operate from unconscious beliefs—I'm too old to learn a new job skill or No one will ever want to be in a relationship with me—without being aware of how they thwart us from even trying certain things. When we are driven by unconscious emotions like fear, sadness, or worry, it can lower our energy and make us feel doomed or overwhelmed, which also hurts our agency.

Deal with your feelings and convictions

Again and again, we work from oblivious convictions—I'm too old to even consider acquiring a new position expertise or Nobody will at any point need to be involved with me—without monitoring how they upset us from attempting certain things. At the point when we are driven by oblivious feelings like dread, bitterness, or stress, it can bring down our energy and cause us to feel bound or overpowered, which likewise harms our organization.

Psychology says it's important to take time for yourself and find clarity. The most important relationship is the one you have with yourself. make it a priority, necessary. Accepting yourself is self care too. there many ways you can practising self care, mentally, physically, spiritually, socially, emotionally, spiritually; always talk positively to yourself

You cannot sit back and wait and expect things to work out for you. steps apply process. if you want to move, you have to move, move, don't let life hold you down, there are times when anything can happen. Sometimes you have to recharge your battery. I refuse to let life swing me, it may be harder. I will become something, something that I will. understanding and knowing that we can create our life the way we want the life we desire that will make us satisfied. I got me here, I can get me out of this.

Don't let your emotions guide you. Life and people have a way to play with our emotions and let them misguide us in many ways. Learn how to make your mind guide you instead of your heart / emotions. I admit that I'm the worst when it comes to decision making, it'll blow my mind trying to think straight, maybe it's because I have a strong complicated mind set or maybe I'm just not good at deciding. A lot of people around us are drowned in their own emotions, their own feelings, not knowing how to get out of the storm. I'm not saying you're not allowed to feel whatever emotion you're feeling. But rather than letting it control you, take over you. You choose to leave, because you don't belong there. I don't know what kind of life you have, but I do know that you can never let your feelings hold back and not enjoy some moments in life.

Simply avoid making decisions when you're very emotional, give yourself time to heal from whatever feeling that's holding you back. Let your feeling get out of you and signal you that you're ready to move on. When you're ready to move on you can then make decisions that you won't regret because you didn't make them under these circumstances where you are sad. Sometimes, I can't think straight, I think about so many things at once which leaves me nothing but confused.

Life has its own way of making feelings of sadness, disappointments, and so many other emotions you have right now they can all disappear within time, and believing that nothing can last forever. Not ever fear of sadness can take your happiness, Moments of joy can be destroyed if you're feeling sad and not being able to be happy.

You don't wanna let anything control you or hold you back from moving on. It's true that how we feel about things have a strong impact on our daily lives/routine. But it can't control us forever. You are a free human being you don't fear feelings just let them be. If you don't like where you are in life, change it. Live your dream don't just dream it. I used to ignore my feelings towards anything if I'm happy. For example, gosh I'm happy today I'm sure something bad would happen. Life teaches you to be strong all by yourself.

We just embrace the life we know.

CONCLUSION

WHAT DO WE DO NOW?

Your future and your present depends on what you are doing now. Are you working hard enough to become what you wanna become? Do you struggle to get up in the morning and still want to be rich? Do you let small actions take over you? Are you letting depression destroy who you are? Do you still dream to lose those couple of pounds you always wanted but you're too lazy to get your butt up and work out? Well, all those questions depend on what you do now to get where you want to, your thoughts, your actions and how you approach things whether you want to be successful and find your ways to get to your dreams or let life choose for you because you're not brave enough to change what you want to change.

You do have the audacity to say to the world that you are here because your journey won't be the same as anyone else's. So, don't let the world tell you what you are looking for. Your voice is heard and you can make an impact on the world you're never going to settle for whatever life has to give you, because you have plans to do, you're strong enough to make those plans and goals come to reality. You're going to learn from every mistake you make to move forward. say goodbye to the people that don't bring positive energy to your life, and start committing to the goals you set and never look back again.

You owe it to yourself to never settle, find something, find your goal work on that goal.

Try to move on from things that bother you, things that distract you so much, get closer to god just you and him alone for some time. allow yourself to cry if you need to, bottle up, when you're bottled up sometimes you explode but eventually you'll start feeling better and ready to move forward.

REFERENCES

https://www. theguardian. com/science/2021/jan/16/inner-voice-self-criticism-psychologist-ethan-kross-chatter-voice-head

https://www. paulamorand. com/uncategorized/do-you-dream-big/ https://blog. usejournal. com/the-real-reason-we-overthink-and-how-to-stop-https://www. psychologytoday. com/intl/blog/the-empowerment-diary/201810/escaping-reality-heal

https://en. wikipedia. org/wiki/Escapism

https://www. psychologytoday. com/us/blog/evil-deeds/200904/anger-disorder-what-it-is-and-what-we-can-do-about-it

https://www. brides. com/protect-your-heart-4169324

https://greatergood. berkeley.edu/article/item/seven ways to feel more in control of your life https:// isaacmorehouse. com/2017/11/30/good-escapism-bad-escapism/ https://www. medicalnewstoday. com/articles/154543

https://www. powerofagency. com/